Rock Your
UGLY CHRISTMAS SWEATER

Anne Marie Blackman &
Brian Clark Howard

RUN
PHIL.

Books published by Running Press are available at special discounts for bulk purchases in the United States by corporations, institutions, and other organizations. For more information, please contact the Special Markets Department at the Perseus Books Group, 2300 Chestnut Street, Suite 200, Philadelphia, PA 19103, or call (800) 810-4145, ext. 5000, or e-mail special.markets@perseusbooks.com.

ISBN 978-0-7624-4473-1
Library of Congress Control Number: 2011942352

E-book ISBN 978-0-7624-4691-9

9   8   7   6   5   4   3   2   1
Digit on the right indicates the number of this printing

Edited by Jordana Tusman
Typography: Burbank, ITC Century, and Girard Script

Running Press Book Publishers
2300 Chestnut Street
Philadelphia, PA 19103-4371

Visit us on the web!
www.runningpress.com

CONTENTS

INTRODUCTION TO UGLY

More colorful than visions of sugarplums and jollier than a sleigh full of inebriated elves, ugly Christmas sweaters are fast becoming a global holiday tradition, celebrated by all ages and walks of life. Tacky Christmas sweaters come in thousands of patterns and an ever-growing array of shapes and sizes, from classic vintage styles from the 1940s and '50s to ugly-yet-sexy sweater dresses, dapper vests, and even showstopping numbers with flashing lights and goofy sound effects.

More and more people are having a blast attending ugly Christmas sweater office parties, family reunions, church gatherings, bar crawls, and charitable benefits. Many attendees even dress strategically, hoping to win the Ugliest Sweater award.

Some of these festive folks may be getting in touch with their inner Bill Cosby, who famously wore garish sweaters with pride on *The Bill Cosby Show*. Others may be channeling Chevy Chase's beloved character from National Lampoon's *Christmas Vacation*. It doesn't matter if you choose to don that hideous "talking moose" ensemble with a sly wink and an ironic grin, or if you sincerely love the way you look in it. There's no judgment here! We have only one rule: the uglier, the better.

We've seen friends share unforgettable evenings on the town, and families laugh out loud together—all while sharing the common bond of ugly holiday sweaters. So make Grandma proud, and break out that colorful Christmas sweater she knitted for you years ago. But never fear. Even if your closets are devoid of ugly goodness, there are thousands of tacky sweaters out there for you to discover. Ask around, hit up garage sales and thrift stores, or visit us at MyUglyChristmasSweater.com.

There's something for every taste and budget, from vintage sweaters that fetch a high price online to recycled outfits pieced together from used Christmas tree skirts and bits of garland. And if Christmas isn't your thing, know that lots of folks are discovering the joys of ugly sweaters themed for Hanukkah and Kwanzaa—even Festivus.

Remember: there is no such thing as being too festive. So string together some popcorn, make yourself some eggnog, sing a few merry tunes—and get ready to rock your ugly Christmas sweater!!

1

GATEWAY TO FESTIVE FUN

Nothing quite says "holiday cheer" like a bright red bow the size of a satellite dish or a sequin-covered Santa and stuffed reindeer that groove to their own sound and light effects. Only we're not talking about a department store display; we're talking about sweaters that *people actually wear*. In public.

Thanks to "ugly Christmas sweater"–themed celebrations, people can wear their holiday cheer on their sleeves—and all over their chests. . . . Whether you get out your glue gun or rediscover that monstrosity your mom wore in 1984, rock your ugly holiday sweater with pride.

Just know that some aficionados have started an arms race of ugly—in hopes of winning bragging rights.

Puff out your chest.
Wear it with confidence.
You own the night.

7

Their parents wonder where they went wrong. This is the day it all began to unravel.

Nothing says "manly rebel" like a cigar, a chopper, some excavating equipment, and a pink poinsettia sweater-vest.

The reverend reminds his congregation of the "reason for the season."

Ack, sensory overload!
But goes to show there's a super-ugly
style for everyone.

These guys sped from zero to ugly in ten seconds flat.

Grandma got all dolled up for a ride in the new set of wheels.

The biggest bow,
with his bro.

It's a sad day when the penny slots hold the key to your Christmas dreams.

And this is what happens when your kid finds your craft closet.

The office hierarchy isn't subtle in the company holiday card.

Merry Christmas
from 1984.

Fun in the romper room.

His prized pink ice skates sweater is lost in a sea of confusion.

A batwing sweater might
have been better suited for flight.

Santa hearts you, too.

He's still deciding where to mount his head.

The Stay Puft, light-up Jack Frost sweater spells victory every time.

Very ready for eight crazy nights.

Jump for joy! It's ugly
Christmas sweater season!

Santa is watching. Now take a seat and behave.

27

Jordan Birch and Chris Boyd threw their first annual ugly Christmas sweater party in Vancouver in 2001, which many credit with kicking off the current international craze. Ugly sweaters: mandatory. Matching T-shirts: optional.

2

CLASSIC VINTAGE UGLY SWEATERS

Let's take a tour with the Ghost of Ugly Christmas Sweaters Past. While tacky holiday sweaters have seen a recent surge in popularity, they have actually been around for quite a while, bringing joy to one and all.

While we can't say for sure that Mary and Joseph rocked them at the first Christmas, we do know they were popular in the 1940s and '50s, and many of those vintage sweaters remain beloved today. These sweaters of yore were usually made with two or three colors, with designs woven into the knits. More often than not, they featured reindeer, moose, and snowflakes, or elements of ski culture.

Over the years, designers reproduced and remixed classic ugly holiday sweaters, but we must never forget the roots of ugly!

An interesting choice of sweater for the job at hand.

Their ugly sweaters, pantaloons, and glasses age them about thirty years.

Dressed in vintage Ralph Lauren, Goliath and his little elf enjoy a quiet evening in the ski chalet.

This kid ha[s]
been ready to [hit]
the slopes
since 1946.

Mini-me Santa turns an idyllic holiday photo creepy.

"I'll hang it right next to the crocheted moose."

Like father,
like son.

Good-bye, dignity.

Props for coordinating beverage of choice with sweater.

Studies have shown that wearing ugly Christmas sweaters before the age of two can cause irreversible damage to one's fashion sense.

It worked in 1955. It works even better today.

Yo, dude.
Diggin' the vest.

Leaping reindeer sweaters offer the conservative crowd something to wear to get into the party.

He had to go to four thrift stores to score this look.

Add a bit of gold fringe to your ~~Hanukkah~~ sweater, and pair it with a set of crutches to really make it pop.

3

EVEN UGLIER SWEATERS FROM THE '80s AND '90s

Over these years, ugly sweaters were produced with more colors, more complex designs, and extra flourishes. In short, they got even uglier.

In the 1980s, bright acrylic sweaters appeared by the rackful, followed by ugly Christmas sweatshirts. It's tempting to think of holiday sweatshirts as the poor man's ugly sweater—but they can be so much more. Many sweaters of the era came with bulky shoulder pads, bat arms, and crafty accents.

For better or worse, the period also saw the rise of the quadrant or grid holiday sweater, in which each square is filled with a different image, such as a teddy bear, rocking horse, or festive dog. Way to multiply the ugly!

Ready to party like it's 1989.

He finally found something to match his favorite turtleneck.

The more you drink,
the uglier it gets.

The inspiration for SantaCon?

Behold the fire-breathing dragon of Christmas.

"Right here, this is Arkansas. Now, any more questions that aren't about my sweater?"

Additional mop supplies located below the hem.

Some doctors know exactly how to put their patients at ease.

As if going to the dentist weren't scary enough.

Peace, joy, and silly silhouettes.

When we think "ugly Christmas sweater party," we immediately think polka.

Happy Kwanzaa from the whitest guy in the room.

The Lucha Libre champion finds his softer side in an '80s knit.

You know you've had one
too many eggnogs if you're petting
the bronze bull.

Santa's homeboy.

6:00 p.m. Buying wine.

11:30 p.m. Out on the town.
This vest gets around.

Ugly sweater slumber party.

Flippin' festive pizza.

Line right up for the ugly
sweater conga.

HOMEMADE HITS AND MISSES

One of the great things about ugly Christmas sweaters is that they can be highly personalized, as unique as snowflakes falling from the heavens. They can show off your sweet knitting skills or push your sewing machine to its limits.

Or you can simply pick up a plain used sweater from a thrift store and add a generous amount of stenciling or a bit of fringe from an old mop. Dig out some felt and googly eyes, and invite the whole family over for an evening of festive crafting. Get out the glue gun, and watch the magic unfold!

We're amazed at what the crafty folks on these pages were able to accomplish with some old holiday ornaments, stuffed animals, sparkling lights, yard clippings, and other odds and ends. Sometimes a little ugly goes a long, long way.

Discount mall
Santa.

"We're gonna need a bigger bow."

Toasting her award from the Red Hat Society.

Ugly winners by leaps and bounds.

What's your man going to wear if you've taken all the bath mat fabric?

Quite possibly the world's ugliest Santa sweaters.

It's Santa's bad dental work that won this duo the Ugliest Couple trophy.

If all you've got is a sprig of holly, you'd better have attitude.

74

This is what you get when your wife puts something together at the last minute.

Yes, he's a tree.
In a Picasso kind of way.

Don't laugh.
He spent
all day on this
thing.

She was super lucky to find the last "brontosaurus eating the star off the Christmas tree" sweater.

They never lose
each other at parties.

He brought a long extension cord so he could mingle.

Baby and Dad think Mom
is a little too into this.

Excellent use of crocheted toilet paper rolls to cover your naughty bits.

We hear boas
are very in this year.

5

BEYOND THE SWEATER: UGLY DRESSES, JACKETS, VESTS, AND MORE

There's certainly no rule that says your ugly holiday outfit has to be a sweater. Lots of folks rock less traditional but equally festive getups, including ugly sweater dresses, vests, jackets, and beyond. The style may change over the years, but the Christmas spirit of glorious ugly remains the same.

And don't forget to accessorize! Ugly Christmas hats, boots, belts, and more can really do wonders to help complete your whole ensemble. You are going for the win, after all! Whatever you choose to wear, it's hard to have a bad time when you're rocking an ugly holiday outfit. Just watch out for that guy with the suspenders and elf ears. Seriously.

Only beautiful people can pull this
look off. Please don't try this at home.

Tested and arrested...

The hostess
with the mostest.
Ornaments, that is.

87

Now there's one more use for those lovely macramé wall hangings.

Consider a holiday sweater set for a more refined look.

Out-blinged by her own palm tree.

"Good morning, Miss Ugly Sweater."

What seemed a
good choice
for the office party
is a bit questionable
at the pump.

Not satisfied
with embroidered bling?
Make it 3-D.

This girl makes even a caftan with balls look sexy.

When you're a radio DJ, you can
get away with wearing anything to work.

What a lucky lady. Her light-up dress attracted the best-looking elf in the room.

A busy vest serves to distract your opponent.

Proudly presenting the twelve dresses of Christmas.
And a little Hanukkah.

She couldn't imagine wearing the same holiday dress more than once.

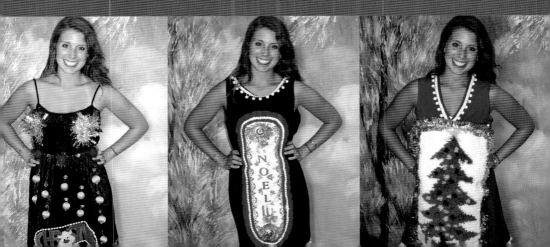

This family has never met a tacky outfit they didn't like.

Wearing an ugly sweatshirt can set you apart from your parents . . . a little.

The invitation said he could bring a date.

6

PETS ROCKING UGLY CHRISTMAS SWEATERS

Not even animals are immune to ugly holiday sweaters. In fact, some of the most outrageous designs have been lovingly reserved specially for kitties and puppies—whether they like it or not. We may never know how Zoi really feels about her Angora sweater, but we think it's just adorable. Now if only we could find her.

If you have a more unusual pet, you aren't off the hook. We've seen some hilarious ugly sweaters on pigs, squirrels, even a pet robot. And horse people? Shoot, they just have more surface area to work with!

But don't worry: no animals (or robots) were harmed in the making of this chapter.

He doesn't appreciate the rarity
of his Cowichan vest.
All he knows is that it's itchy.

Remain calm.
The ASPCA is on the way.

Nothing says "festive" like cats and a sock puppet.

Kitty isn't finding this nearly as funny.

They may look tough, but
they love dress-up day at the kennel.

Who says dogs don't get
embarrassed?

Someone's ready for bed.

Tree skirts are one-size-fits-all:
tree, man, beast.

You can see it in his eyes.
He's had quite enough of Christmas.

'Tis the season to celebrate with your sow.

Little rodent sweaters.
Coming to a store near you.

Show off your ripped bod with
a form-fitted vest, or hide your rolls with
a roomy Nordic number.

Little Tommy was okay with the photo shoot until the bearded cat showed up.

Zoi wonders why
an indoor cat
has to put up with this
sweater crap.

They love their Scottie.
We're just not sure the feeling's mutual.

All the other dogs at temple are
going to be jealous.

Vinnie: the incredible levitating cat of her dreams.

The captain bears a striking resemblance to his first mate.

"I'm supposed to take orders from the girl in the crazy shirt?"

How lucky to find a dog to match your sweater.

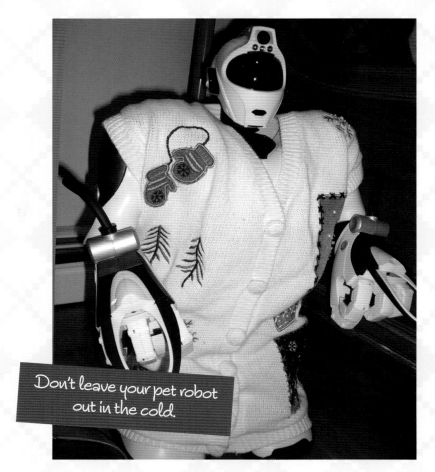

Don't leave your pet robot out in the cold.

7

WINTER WONDERLAND . . . OF UGLY

Beyond celebrating the holidays, some people like to don ugly sweaters because they crave the warmth and emotional comfort they provide. Fortunately, there are plenty of wintry designs to choose from, from serene snowy scenes to adorable Arctic animals.

Ugly sweaters also make great gear for winter activities, as some of the following pages will show. What better way to draw attention to your band, wash a fire truck, distract the opposing hockey team, or stand out on the slopes than by wearing a sweater that screams all kinds of ugly?

Thumbs up if you love snow!

Over the river and through the woods to Grandmother's house we go.

Taking Mom's sweater out
for a spin.

Acrylic knits make for eye-catching skiwear.

That's <u>Mrs.</u> Frosty,
thank you very much.

The party doesn't begin until the truck has been washed.

X-rated ugly.

Ugly yoga king dancer pose.

His waterlogged knit really dragged him down.

Varsity Team Tacky.

Best to wear a
helmet when
pirouetting in Mom's
XXL vest.

Gather 'round the Festivus pole.

FESTIVUS
for the rest of us

A tutu and ugly sweater are the perfect accessories for a day on the slopes.

In their fringed sweaters, this hockey team intimidates their opponents.

Some musicians really know how to rock the ugly.

She'd be happy all day wearing her Bullwinkle hat.

And the angel
said unto
them:
"Get thine ugly!"

ROCK CHRISTMAS IN JULY

It seems that some people love their ugly Christmas sweaters so much that they just can't keep them in storage. Even if it's ninety degrees outside, they'll sweat through the heat in order to show off their tacky goods.

Of course, December is hot in the Southern Hemisphere, but it's also true that more and more people are getting into the holiday spirit on July 25 to celebrate "Christmas in July." Fortunately for these folks, there is an increasing array of "ugly sweater" T-shirts and baseball caps. We have even seen brave souls hit the board-walks and beaches in breathable sweater-vests. To our great dismay, we haven't seen many ugly holiday skirts or shorts, but we'd like to believe it's only a matter of time now.

Take the ugly plunge!
It's Christmas in July!

147

So ugly they forced him to walk the plank.

"Ahoy. Merry, merry. I'm thrilled they made me wear this."

Collars are optional on the course today.

"Come on in,
the water's fine."

Funny Hat Day in the Sun Belt.

The only thing they caught that day was grief.

Even the toughest tats can be tamed with a poinsettia vest.

A salute to ugly Christmas sweaters everywhere.

Hang 10!
And wear a vest to
keep the sun
off your back.

When this guy goes clamming, Frosty always has his back.

Just because your ugly "sweater" T-shirt says "golf" doesn't mean you'll be allowed on the course.

Don't mess with the ugly Christmas sweater mafia.

Urban ugly.

Must be
Ugly Sweater
Day at the
yacht club.

A child's size is always a good choice.

Did that bird
just poop
on my
sweater-vest?

162

Not the most practical water-wear, but oh so festive!

If you're trying to reduce glare, wearing a bright sweater probably won't help.

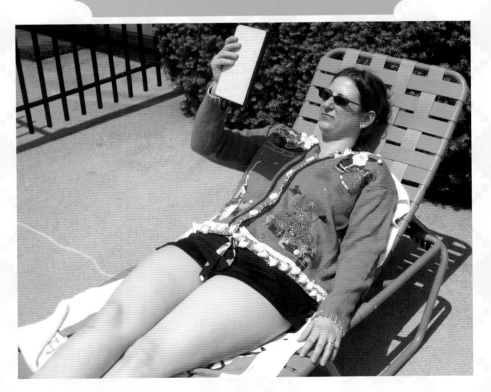

Jammin'
ugly sweater style.

165

After exhausting his job options, he found employment as a snowman-juggling unicyclist.

9

WEAR IT TO WIN IT: THE BEST OF THE BEST

We searched high and low to bring you the most outrageously ugly sweaters we could find, and we can say with experience that rocking one of these numbers is certain to make you the life of any party. There's even a good chance you'll get more requests for photos than the mall Santa.

If you're on a budget and can't afford to order a custom über-ugly sweater online, don't despair. Get a used sweater and pick up a string of LED holiday lights from the drugstore, or pin on some old ornaments, silly stuffed animals, or whatever else you can find around your holiday tree. Bragging rights could soon be yours.

Someday the kids will regret this.

"What are the chances we'd show up in the same outfit?"

It doesn't matter how cute you are. A Santa Sasquatch vest is still ugly.

Good thing their sweaters light up. They'll need them to help navigate.

Just pile the presents around her.

Now he has
an angel complex.

Rudolph called. He wants his
light-up antlers back.

Dad really seems to be enjoying his retirement in the country.

Sometimes they're ugly enough right off the rack.

Ironic?

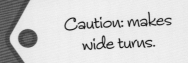
Caution: makes wide turns.

Should we be laughing at your sweater or your elf underpants?

Why is it that the biggest guy always insists on the most obnoxious sweater?

They may not agree on politics, but
they do agree on ugly.

So this moose
walks into a bar…

Although the pink cap is a
nice touch, they really should have
sprung for Santa hats.

Holiday flow
from head to toe.

Just hanging around the ol' Christmas tree.

Now cars can
see him
coming from a
mile away.

His singing, dancing 3-D sweater won the gold.

A toast to beautiful ugly sweaters everywhere!

CONTRIBUTORS

Front cover: Jason Yormark (left), Zacfisherphoto.com (center), Alli Valentine (right); back cover: Jordan Birch and Chris Boyd, Co-founders & Hosts of The 10th Annual Ugly Christmas Sweater Party in Vancouver Canada, the original trendsetter. www.uglychristmassweaterparty.ca Property of Big Knits Inc.; page 7: Jason Yormark; pages 8, 57: Katie Knutson; page 9: Buck Evans; pages 10, 11, 12, 15, 24, 27, 30, 32, 33, 34, 35, 36, 37, 42 (bottom), 45, 46, 48, 49, 50, 51, 52, 54, 62, 63, 67, 68, 69, 70, 75, 79, 86, 88, 91, 92, 93, 98, 99, 100, 101, 104, 106, 107, 109, 111, 113, 118, 121, 122, 129, 130, 131, 133, 135, 136, 137, 140, 141, 144, 145, 147, 148, 149, 163 (right), 165, 166, 168, 169, 171, 172, 173, 175, 177, 178 (bottom), 181, 182, 183: Anne Marie Blackman, MyUglyChristmasSweater.com; pages 13, 90, 110, 123, 151, 152, 153, 154, 178 (top): January Meyer; page 14: Nick DeLong; page 16: Lisa Stevens; page 17: Natalie Venuto, Natalievenuto.com, @natalievenuto; page 18: Zacfisherphoto.com; pages 19, 20, 128: Dom & Tom; pages 21, 41, 43, 60, 61, 94, 97, 158, 159, 162, 163 (left), 186, 187, 188: Brian Clark Howard; page 22: Christian Ramirez photograph of Jeff Yanc for The Loft Cinema; pages 23, 185: Caroline Wheeler; pages 25, 127: Zachary Cobb, Westside Studio; page 26: Derek Henderson; page 28: Jordan Birch and Chris Boyd, co-founders and hosts of The Annual Ugly Christmas Sweater Party in Vancouver Canada, Uglychristmassweaterparty.ca, Property of Big Knits Inc.; page 31: Leila Anne, Flickr; page 38: Sheila Longo and Corey Sullivan; page 39: David Douglass; page 40: Tasha, Bygumbygolly.com; pages 42 (top), 87: Dana Ramirez; pages 47, 155, 157: Jim Smith; page 53: Robin Hayden; pages 55, 134: Nate Anderson; page 56: Photograph of The Polkaholics by Vera Gavrilovic; page 58: John Carleton, Futureman.us; page 59: Allan and Diana Howard; page 64: Freedom Moreno; pages 66, 150: Kcsweaterparty.com; pages 71, 78: Mandy Jouan; page 72: Marco Repola; page 73 (top): Misty Hume; page 73 (bottom): ebeegrn, Flickr; page 74: Greene's 2009; page 76: Rosina Thom; page 77: Damon Jasso; page 80: H. Sterling Cross; pages 81, 83, 184: Coolestfamilyontheblock.com; page 82: David Bechle; page 85: Mickyhoogen.com/Mickysees.com; page 89: Daniel Woolf Photography; pages 95, 164: Lisa Bickford; page 96: Stacey Yonkus; page 102: Angie Eason; page 105: Liz Kearley; page 108: Mayra E. Sedano; page 112: Alli Valentine; page 114: Jon Sauder; page 115: Rebecca Buckley; page 116: Katherine Cundiff Photography; page 117: Dana Watters; page 119: Beth Lind; page 120: Shannon Pedit; page 124: radmike; page 125: Andrew Kjellman; page 132: Jim Spernyak; page 138: Cooper Rowing Club; pages 139, 142: Karin Mullins; page 143: Britt Ernst, Britternst.com; page 156: Rich McGarry; page 160: Leo Costantino; page 161: Greg Foster and Lisa Miyake, Baadsheep.com; page 170: Madaline Andre; page 174: Jeffrey Gray; page 176: Chuck Webster; page 179: Nicole Holovinsky; page 180: Leonard Balistreri; page 189: Eden Folwell

ACKNOWLEDGMENTS

We thank our editor, Jordana Tusman, our designer, Jason Kayser, and the rest of the Running Press team, who made this project a wonderful experience. Thanks also to our agent, David Fugate of Launch Books, who believed in this project from the beginning.

Anne Marie Blackman

Thanks to my coauthor, Brian Clark Howard, for being a fan of my ugly sweaters and for partnering with me on this project. Brian is a talented writer who is a pleasure to work with, and I thank him for his expertise in making the idea for this book a reality.

Thanks to my husband, Jim Blackman, and my sons, Colton and Austin, for their support, ideas, and occasional modeling. Thanks to my parents, Paul and Maureen Burns, my brother, Paul Burns, and my sister, Beth Burns, for all their love and laughter. Thanks to all my friends and family, especially my Killington, Vermont, neighbors, whose spirit, generosity, and love of a good joke are extraordinary. I am blessed to have you all in my life.

Thanks to Ramsey Mohsen and Zachary Cobb, January Meyer, Micky Hoogendijk, and all the MyUglyChristmasSweater.com customers who shared their holiday photos.

Brian Clark Howard

I thank my coauthor, Anne Marie Blackman, who invited me to work on this book, knowing we share an appreciation for ugly sweaters. Anne Marie has an impressive work ethic, an infectious sense of humor, and an impeccable eye for ugly. Thanks to Ed Scheff of MSN and Dan Shapley of The Daily Green, who first suggested I write about ugly Christmas sweaters.

Thanks to my friends and family, many of whom appear in this book. Thank you for digging out dusty photos and musty sweaters and posing for the camera. Thanks especially to Corey Yoquelet, Bayard Russell, Dave Stiasny, Martin Meisenheimer, Susan Sotardi, Lisa and Andy Bickford, Amy Fosnot, Allan and Diana Howard, the Townsquare Media crew, and Gloria Dawson.

Finally, thanks to everyone else who shared photos and happy memories with us. You inspire us all.